Skoob Books Publishing Ltd., **London** presents a new imprint:

Skoob *PACIFICA* is contributing to World Literatures in English, disseminating regional literatures of the Pacific Rim and promoting understanding between continents.

At the turn of the last century, Europe developed a penchant for novels set in lands afar which had a tendency to look **at** the colonies whereas the Postcolonials view from within themselves, experimenting with the deviation from tradition and affirming the aesthetic of the sublime as against an aesthetic of the beautiful.

"The reality of cultural entity should be the simultaneous act of eliciting from history, mythology, and literature, for the benefit of both genuine aliens and the alienated, a continuing process of self-apprehension whose temporary dislocation appears to have persuaded many of its non-existence or its irrelevance (= retrogression, reactionarism, racism, etc.) in contemporary world reality."
Wole Soyinka, *Nobel Laureate*

"Storytelling, to the readers of a *genre* of novel, written by a particular writer for a small group of people in a large and fragmented culture, still survives in those places the English like to call the Commonwealth. This idea of narration, of the active voice is in the calypsonian as the ballad singer, the narrator, the political satirist."
Derek Walcott, *Nobel Laureate*

As the *fin-de-millenium* approaches, the colonies have a voice of their own, a new *genre* has developed. Ironically, this diachrony is written in the language of the Imperialist. Behind the facade of tropical, sandy beaches and factories of video games lies the cross-cultural and interliterary tradition o⸍ ⸍⸍⸍ ⸍⸍⸍⸍⸍⸍⸍⸍

Skoob *PACIFICA: THE EM*

GW00689778

SKOOB *Pacifica* SERIES

Joint Series Editors: Ms. C.Y. Loh & Mr. I.K. Ong

Available Titles

2000 **Skoob PACIFICA Anthology No. 1:** *S.E. Asia Writes Back !*

2001 **K.S. Maniam** - The Return

2002 **Wong Phui Nam** - Ways of Exile: *Poems from the First Decade*

2003 **K.S. Maniam** - In a Far Country

2011 **Ramli Ibrahim** - In the Name of Love, a play in three Flushes

Forthcoming Winter 1993/94

2013 **Skoob PACIFICA Anthology No.2:** *The Pen is Mightier than the Sword*

2005 **Salleh Ben Joned** - Amok ! the play

2004 **Latiff Mohidin** - Selected Poems, a bilingual edition

2007 **Chin Woon Ping** - Shaman Myths, Poems & Prose

Forthcoming Spring/Summer 1994

2006 **Kee Thuan Chye** - (A Play, Poems and Essays)

2008 **Thor Kah Hoong** - Telling Tales

2009 **Robert Yeo** - (A Play, Poems & Essays)

2010 **Arthur Yap** - Collected Poems

2012 **Karim Raslan** - The Bendaharas

2014 **Shirley Geok-lin Lim** - Writing S.E. Asia in English: Against the Grain, *a literary criticism*

2015 **Shirley Geok-lin Lim** - Modern Secrets: *Selected Poems*

SKOOB *acifica* SERIES

No. 2011

IN THE NAME OF LOVE
An Insight in Three Flushes

Acknowledgements

The Author would like to acknowledge the assistance and support of the following people: James Murdoch, Chu Li, Sabera Shaik, Ramli Hassan, André Berly, Henry Barlow, Norazizah Ibrahim, Norina Yahya, Bernice Chauly and Dolores S.

Ramli Ibrahim

IN THE NAME OF LOVE
An Insight in Three Flushes

Introduction

by

Professor John McRae
University of Nottingham

SKOOB BOOKS PUBLISHING
LONDON

Copyright © Ramli Ibrahim 1993
All Rights Reserved
Introduction © Professor John McRae
Cover Painting © Latiff Mohidin
Cover © Allan Kwok
Photographs of Ramli Ibrahim and Sabera Shaik © Chu Li

First published in 1993 by
SKOOB BOOKS PUBLISHING LTD.
Skoob *PACIFICA* Series
11A-17 Sicilian Avenue
off Southampton Row and
Bloomsbury Square
London WC1A 2QH
Fax: 71-404 4398

ISBN 1 871438 24 1

Agents:
Skoob Books (Malaysia) Sdn. Bhd.
11 Jalan Telawi Tiga, Bangsar Baru,
59100 Kuala Lumpur
Tel/Fax: 603-255 2686

Graham Brash (Pte) Ltd.
32 Gul Drive,
Singapore 2262
Tel: 65-861 1336, 65-862 0437.
Fax: 65-861 4815

Typeset by Pearly Kok . Tel/Fax: 603-255 2686
Printed by Polygraphic, Malaysia. Fax: 603-905 4851

for

Asri

The characters in these plays are composites inspired by many real and fictitious characters with no claim to be a portrait of any one particular person.

In the Name of Love was first performed by Sabera Shaik in Kuala Lumpur on 1st December, 1991, as part of *Pesta Sutra 1991, Up To You !*

Contents

Page

An Introduction by Professor John McRae   xi

FIRST FLUSH: The Makyong Actress
Background Notes   3
MAK SU - The Malay Version (on verso)   6
MAK SU - The English Version (on recto)   7

SECOND FLUSH: The Dance-Mother
Brief Notes on the Character   45
SARASA   47

THIRD FLUSH: The Food Lover
Background Notes   59
DEENA   61

INTRODUCTION

by
JOHN McRAE
University of Nottingham

Ramli Ibrahim is known world-wide as a unique figure in the dance; one who combines classical and modern, Eastern and Western, equally at home in Sadler's Wells Theatre in London, in Sydney, where he made his name as the star of the Sydney Dance Company, and at the shrine of Indian classical dance, at Kalashetra, on the outskirts of Madras.

In some ways it is surprising that such a figure should move into the drama of the spoken word. Indeed it might be considered both risky and arrogant for a man whose medium is movement with music to venture where other writers in his native Malaysia have had more than a little difficulty in finding an audience. But Ramli has written for many years - the move into theatrical writing is a natural development of the cultural concerns he has expressed in many articles on a wide range of controversial themes.

In the Name of Love is a linked series of three plays for a single actress. The three characters are respectively known as Mariam Titisan Airmata or Mak Su, a Makyong actress, Sarasa, "the Dance-Mother", and Deena, "the Food Lover", whose main compensation in life since her British colonel husband was murdered is what she eats.

Although focusing on one single character in each mono-drama, taken together, the plays touch on an immense range of themes: from the loss of the Makyong theatrical troupe tradition in Kelantan and Terengganu, through the anguish of vicarious ambition, again in a theatrical context, to the colonial woman caught during the unrest of the emergency period and victim of the struggle for independence who is also a victim of the violence of modern political struggle.

The subtitle of the work, *An Insight in Three Flushes*, is indicative of the writer's intentions. All the women are growing old alone whether married, like Sarasa and Mak Su, or widowed, like Deena. Their ages range from early fifties through sixties to about sixty eight. The "flushes" from menopausal to post-menopausal and "elderly" are an insight, not only into female frustration, but into concerns of art, (central to Mak Su), dependence and self-deception, cultural and racial interaction, and the essential loneliness of outsiders.

The three characters are among the unconsidered, the forgotten cast-offs of the modern world. Heroines they are not - at least in any conventional sense. But given Ramli's enduring concerns with the recovery of Malaysian cultural traditions, Mak Su is very much some kind of hero, embodying as she does so many of the representative elements of the traditional, universal "rogue and vagabond" Makyong theatre which even in Shakespeare's day was not necessarily approved of by officialdom: the travelling players, gender-swapping roles, popular appeal, music and dance. Makyong theatre, whose decline Mak Su bewails, is any cultural phenomenon in decline or fallen into destitution; Mak Su herself, an artist who sees a new generation trampling on the traditions she has done so much to nourish. The loss is of the same carnivalesque spirit of celebration and affirmation of humanity that Mikhail Bakhtin traced in the culture of late medieval Europe; it never will be completely lost, but is eternally on the verge of disappearing into the void. It constantly needs a Mak Su to remind us of what we are in danger of losing, so that the carnivalesque can be reclaimed.

The genuine sense of loss in *Mak Su* is gently (or perhaps not so gently) pointed up by the parody of Indian movie acting "with exaggerated melodrama, breast beating, hair pulling and wailing" in *Sarasa*. The contrast between the knowing, self-possessed, workaday Mak Su and the dowdiness and whinging ways of Sarasa is neatly underscored in the music used: Mak Su revels in the songs from her beloved Makyong tradition; Sarasa has as the accompaniment to her whining and raving "Indian Film Music - the cheap and common variety." The falsity of Sarasa's vicarious ambitions, as she pushed her daughter Komala through endless singing and dancing lessons, is in poignant contrast to the selflessness and dedication, the unselfpitying vitality of Mak Su. Ramli clearly loves the character Mak Su and gives her the most fully expansive personality of the three, as she reminisces, unfolding her art (to Ramli himself, addressed as Li, the unseen interlocutor, the young artist whose work will celebrate that art). Mariam of the Teardrops she may be, but there is a joyousness in what she remembers and how she remembers it, a tempering of the deep regret of loss. The Makyong theatre still continues to be the most positive presence in her life, even in the reduced circumstances of cultural and political exile.

Sarasa has nothing to mitigate her loss; her daughter is gone for ever, lost to ambition and to family as she elopes with the son of her family's worst enemy. And where Mak Su is supremely conscious of her audience, her unseen interlocutor, Sarasa cannot see that she is a parody of herself, a mockery of the artistic standards she has failed so miserably to understand.

Deena's situation is more complex. Widowed as a result of violence she is still expiating, she inhabits a space she rules, but which is in fact a non-space, an inter-cultural vacuum. If Sarasa recalls something of *Romeo and Juliet* in the parent's failure to comprehend an offspring's love for a family enemy, Deena recalls Duke Ferdinand's words in *Measure for Measure*, "Thou hast neither youth nor age, But as 'twere an after-dinner sleep dreaming on both." She has never been able to enjoy youth or age to the full, but she has mastered an art - the art of living in and controlling her own space. Her obsession with food is a consolation, substitute and displacement of grief and guilt, and self-devouring creativity, all at the same time. Like Mak Su and Sarasa she has lost the world she knew, in which she felt secure, and now lives on her memories. She is conscious of her 'role', of the strangeness of her position outside society and its norms. She is conscious therefore of the impression she will make on her audience, her listeners, and is gently self-mocking in that awareness.

Although they are monodramas the plays are therefore almost dialogic in their establishing of involvement between character and audience. Sarasa has a husband at whom she can direct her vindictive self-dramatizings. The other two women prefer to take their listeners into their confidence. It is this sharing of experience which makes the plays a successful exploration of the emotional heartlands they depict: each play reflects and refracts images of the other two to make a coherent integrated whole. And the whole contains enough historical and cultural material to stand almost as a metaphor for the cultural state of his native land as Ramli Ibrahim sees it.

Great care has been taken with the language the characters use. In both the original Malay (Bahasa Malaysia) version of *Mak Su* and in the other two plays, written in English, the language is a clear indicator of status in terms of race, education and social standing.

Sarasa "speaks in pidgin, ungrammatical and colloquial Malaysian-English." If language is power, linguistic exclusion is here an emblem of disempowerment. Mak Su's language is, in contrast, funny, interactive, and highly personal in its idiolect and dialect. Her constant use of interjections, such as *"Lah!"* and *"Kan?"* allows for a musicality, a dialogic dance with expression and ejaculation which gestures and the actress's performance skills will bring to vivid life.

Deena's reflections are couched in the most Anglicised English, with the most modern cultural references which lapse inevitably into the language of historic loss: only the language (and action) of self-indulgence can compensate for the harsh reality that history represents.

This range of language and richness of character are the perfect representation of the racial, cultural and historical mix that is present-day Malaysia. Tension is never far below the surface in these plays. There is a range of binaries and dichotomies pulling against one another: present and past, traditional and contemporary, provincial and city, violence and tolerance, insider and outsider.

As Aijaz Ahmad usefully reminds us in *In Theory* (1992), it is very dangerous to work with "the nation/culture equation, whereby all that is indigenous becomes homogenized into a single cultural formation which is then presumed to be necessarily superior to the capitalist culture which is identified discretely with the 'West' and the tradition/modernity binary, whereby each can be constructed in a discrete space and one or the other is adopted or discarded." *In the Name of Love* is about plurality of experience, locally set but universally accessible.

Ramli Ibrahim, in his life as an artist, displays some of the insider/outsider dichotomy the play as a whole embodies; he is a Malay whose art has evolved from a cultural frame of reference which is world-wide. The artist is always something of an outsider, and very often something of a subversive. Ramli's art rises above national and nationalistic constraints, affirming the artist as individual and as citizen of the world, a world which has to accommodate violence (graphically so in Deena's case) but which can save itself with humour, with art, with commitment.

What Ramli has done in these three plays is remarkable on several counts. Not only does he reveal a glorious capacity to write touchingly and wittily - which we had no right to expect from South East Asia's greatest dancer and master of physical expression - but he handles vast themes of love and loss, tradition and art, time and talent in ways that are accessible, original, and entirely true to the cultural roots of present-day Malaysia.

Any actress would kill to play these roles: the Western reader might like to imagine an impossible amalgam of Maggie Smith, Dawn French and Alan Bennett in order to capture the spirit, the theatrical vitality and the subversive humour of the plays.

When the English version of *Mak Su* was first performed in a reading by Ramli himself at Universiti Pertanian Malaysia, the audience's positive response was immediate: the laughter of recognition, involvement with character and emotions, identification with the cultural and emotional issues, and enjoyment of a marvellously idiosyncratic way of rendering the local dialect into the universal language of self-justification. This is daring theatre, taking risks and living dangerously, reviving a spirit that at the same time subverts and affirms the cultural concerns it displays, questioning and challenging, but never losing sight of that essential theatrical quality: entertainment. The play marks a major contribution to South East Asian theatre, and one which will delight audiences anywhere.

FIRST FLUSH

MAK SU
The Makyong Actress

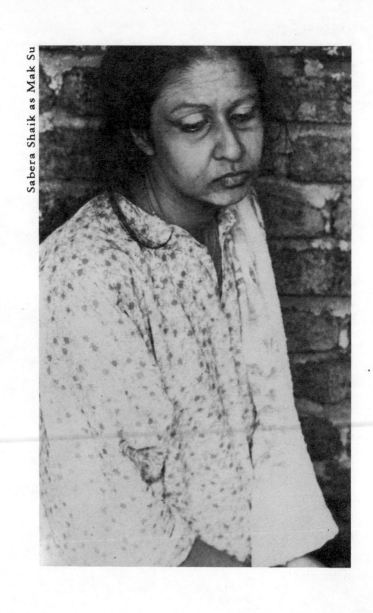

Sabera Shaik as Mak Su

Background Notes

Scenario:

The time is the present; the place a remote fishing village somewhere in Trengganu. The Makyong, an ancient traditional theatre form, is dying. The present society no longer finds it relevant to support such itinerant artists, not even granting them the dignity of dying gracefully. There is also a recent law banning performances in Kelantan, the state of its origin, spurred by Islamic revisionist policies.

Sound:

A small transistor-cassette player.

At some point the radio plays some typical old Malay favourites of the Fifties - an R. Azmi (an old Malay crooner) song, for example.

Sound effects will need to include the sound of the sea and a short bursts of thunder, lightning and rain, sounds that signify East Coast of the Peninsula.

Also required is a recording of a Makyong performance, say, of the *Menghadap Rebab*. This will be trailed off in an evocative composition that captures the essence of Makyong, at the same time alluding to the passing away of a cherished tradition as Mak Su retreats into the world of her past.

Structure:

Mak Su, a prima donna of Makyong, is an elderly woman in her late sixties. Mak Su is caught by surprise at the sudden appearance of her visitor whom she has not seen for a long time. She has just been drying cuttlefish by the beach. She is slightly embarrassed. Her house is a dingy shanty. She brushes her dress, repairs her dishevelled hair in an attempt to make herself more presentable. Finally she sits down to converse with her visitor.

Mak Su is feeling slightly down. She has just recovered from an illness which resulted in her missing the chance to perform overseas, an opportunity of a lifetime. She finds out that some of her other Makyong contemporaries, less talented and well-known, have just left for an overseas tour. She is irritated by the whole thing and becomes a little bit of a sour grapes.

The conversation then shifts to the heyday of Makyong during her time. Mak Su eventually unfolds her art, the centre of her being and her concept of *angin* and *rasa*. With Mak Su, when she is taken over by her *angin*, *'malu'* (inhibition or shame) has no place in her sense of self.

Mak Su is given a tape recording of a recent performance. She listens and is overtaken by the magic of the performance and the nostalgia it evokes. She is in her own world. One is left with the impression that Mak Su, in spite of her material poverty, is at peace with herself, a fulfilled being who has found release in her art.

MAK SU

Scene:
The transformation of the actress into the person of Mak Su happens on stage behind a back-lit screen.

Sound:
As Mak Su is being prepared, her favourite song is being played, an old R. Azmi favourite of the Fifties.

The screen is taken away, revealing Mak Su in a pose - a typical village woman looking beyond the audience into the middle distance.

Black Out.
Stage lights together with a typical Malay tune that one normally hears on the radio when a 'kampong' scene is evoked as Mak Su emerges - most probably from the kitchen. She is slightly dishevelled. She is surprised to see her visitor.

MAK SU
The Malay version

Eh Li! Bila sampai? Tak royak dengan Mak Su nak mari. Mana Mak Su nak tau. Mak Su baru naik dari pantai ni. Jemor sotong. Kain baju ni masih lagi bau sotong!

Kalau khabar siang nak mari, boleh Mak Su masakkan tupat sotong. Ni datang macam malaikat tiba tiba ja. Mana nak ada masa.

Hah mari duduk Li. Mari. *(She switches off the transistor. She brings out a mat for her visitor.)*

Tau kau Li apa tu tupat sotong? Oi sedap tupat sotong tu. Masakan spesel sini. Kat Kelumpur tak kan ada orang buat. Mana nak rasa tupat sotong?

Ah - pulut di gaul dengan santan, kemudian sumbatkan dalam sotong. Lepas tu masaklah. Ha, serai jangan lupa. Bila Li datang sekali lagi boleh Mak Su masakkan nanti.

Nampaknya tak dok apa yang boleh Mak Su hidangkan. Ayer teh ajalah nampaknya.

(She brushes her sleeves and disapproves of her appearance. She disappears and reappears with a tray of tea.)

Ugh. Mak Su busuk bango bau sotong!

MAK SU

Eh Li! When you got here? Just like you. Never let me know you are coming today. How can I know? I just got back from the beach - drying *sotong* [1]. Still smell of the damn squid!

Now, if you warned me you're coming today, I'd prepare you *tupat sotong* [2]. But you just appear suddenly like this - like a *malaikat* [3]! Where got time to do it?

Eh, why stand outside? Come now! Come in! *(She switches off the transistor radio. She brings out a mat for her visitor.)*

Ah, never heard before what is *tupat sotong*, right? Oi, its delicious! It's our special here! Bet you nobody in *Kelumpur* [4] knows how to make it. Then how to know its taste?

Simple to make! Ah - glutinous rice, mix with coconut milk. Stuff it in the *sotong* Then cook*lah!* Ha, don't forget the lemon grass. Ah, never mind - next time. I'll make it for you when you come again.

Looks like nothing much I can serve you today. Plain tea *sajalah!* [5]

(She brushes her sleeves and disapproves of her appearance. She disappears and reappears with a tray of tea.)

Ugh! How I stink of sotong!

---

1 cuttlefish
2 stuffed cuttlefish
3 angel
4 Kuala Lumpur
5 only

Ala. Dari tak buat gapo gapo. Baik Mak Su kerjakan sotong tu. Bukan susah sangat.

Modal nya pun modal tokeh Li! Mak Su beli ja sotong basah dari tokeh tu. Sotong tu Mak Su basuh dengan air laut - buang kotor kotor dia. Kemudian baru jemur kat pantai. Lepas tu jual balik ke tokeh. Tolaklah modal tadi.

Tak banyak mana untung Li! Maklumlah. Bila dah kering - hai, berat nya pun berapa sangat?

Le ni pun bukan ada gapo gapo sangat. Dah bebulan bulan tak main Makyong.

Dua minggu lepas ada Mak Su main petri di kampung dekat kemp ashkar tu. Ada orang sakit. Tu lah caranya sekarang ni...

Apa lagi Mak Su kau nak buat.

(Mak Su takes a tin of cigarettes, opens it and smokes one.)

Ku Ismail tak main Mak Yong doh. Kalau main boleh se sen dua.

Ala, just look at me. How not to do anything? Better for me to do something useful. Working on the *sotong* is not that difficult, Li!

No need to worry about capital. It's all arranged with the *tokeh*. [6] I buy the *sotong* from him. Clean the lot inside out. Wash them in the sea and then dry the stuff! By the beach*lah!* After that, I sell back to the same *tokeh*. He will *kerat* [7] from what I bought first.

Ala Li! What profit, I ask you? *Sotong!* How much will they weigh when dried?

Hai, what to do? As it is, there's nothing much else I can do around here. *Tak main* [8] Makyong for months!

Two weeks ago there was *main petri* [9] at the village near the military camp. A man was sick. But you'll starve if you depend on people calling you for these things. They don't ask for us anymore. Not like those days.

Nothing I can do. Well - that's now it is now...

(Mak Su takes a tin of cigarettes, opens it and smokes one.)

Even Ku Smail got no interest to *main* [10] Makyong nowadays. That time I could earn a little bit here and there from his troupe.

---

6 Chinese middleman
7 deduct
8 Haven't performed
9 shamanistic genre
10 perform

Takkanlah nak duduk kat pintu siang tunggu, malam tunggu. Dok tenguk matahari turun naik...

(By this time, Mak Su has seated herself comfortably. She unties her hair and ties it again tightly in a high bun. She lights herself a cigarette.)

Pak Soh kau?

Hai Pak Soh kau pergi ka Marang. Tengah hari kang baliklah dia. Dia pergi mintak pitih main wayang kelmarin.

Belum dapat dapat lagi. Dah dua bulan masih lagi orang tu tak bayar bayar.

Hai bukan banyak sangat. Tolak sini sana, dapatlah tiga empat puluh. Jadilah Li. Dari tak dok!

Apa kau kata? Rombongan Makyong tu dah bertolak ke Merika?

Si Jah tu pun pergi sama?

Si Jah tu memang gatal benar nak pergi luar negeri. Hmm biarlah dia pergi. Nanti kat sana diniaya orang, sakit pening...

You tell me, what is there for me to do? Wait at the *serambi* [11] and watch the sun go up and down? Day in, day out? Wait for work to find me?

(By this time, Mak Su has seated herself comfortably. She unties her hair and ties it again tightly in a high bun. She lights herself a cigarette.)

Your Pak Soh?

Hai, your Pak Soh gone to Marang. Back in the afternoon, most probably. He's gone to ask those people for his *wayang* [12] money.

Hasn't received it yet. So late. Two months ago he played. Still hasn't been paid yet.

Hai, not much Li! When you *tolak* [13] the other expenses, he'll end up thirty or forty ringgit in his pocket. Better than nothing, Li!

Apa dia? [14] That Makyong troupe gone to *Merika* [15] already?

That Jah gone with them too?

Hai, that Jah - *gatal* [16] to go to foreign country. *Biarkan* [17] - let the woman go. Wants so much to travel that bitch. Let her

---

11 verandah
12 Shadow play
13 deduct
14 What's that?
15 America
16 itching
17 Let (her) be!

mana tau. Ah siapa nak jaga? Mau sangat tenguk negeri orang. Rasakanlah dia nanti!

Apa? Gambar Si Jah tubik surat khabar kau kata?

Mana? Mari Mak Su kau tenguk.

Mm...Kesian. Pakai kain pelekat ja dia!

Teruk betul Si Jah tu. Hai, kalau ia pun, tak boleh ke pakai kain yang gak berseri sikit kalau nak ambil gambar tu. Itulah dia Si Jah. Teruk! Kalau kat kampung ni, seminggu kadang kadang podar pun tak sentuh muka. Orang darat benar Si Jah tu! Mak Su tau benar dia tu!

Dia orang memang nak Mak su pergi sama. Mak Su sakit masa tu. Masa dok panggil latihan tu Mak Su terlempar sakit. Sampai orang ingat Mak Su dah sampai masa agaknya.

Ini pun Mak Su bukan sihat sangat.

Ah kalau pergi pun siapa nak jaga Si Abang cucu Mak Su tu. Dia masih sekolah lagi. Pak Soh kau jugak. Siapa nak jaga mereka?

do it. *Kena nanti!* [18] The suffering, illness - who knows what else... Who wants to look after her there? That woman simply can't wait to go oversea! Let her! Let's see how she survives the trip.

What you say? Her photo appeared in the newspaper?

Where? Let your Mak Su see!

Tsk tsk... Just look at her - a pitiful sight, don't you think? Wearing a simple kain *pelekat* [19] in public! No pride at all this Jah!

What to do? Not her fault - she's just a peasant, this Jah.

Hai, tell me Li. If you know you are going to appear in a newspaper - wouldn't you wear something a little bit nicer? Instead of a drab kain *pelekat*. Well, what did I tell you about her. She is incredible! Sometimes when she is in the *kampung* [20] - for a week she won't powder her face! A real *darat* [21] this Jah. I know her too well!

Actually Li, they wanted me to come too. But that time, I was very, very ill. They called for rehearsal. But what to do? I was flat on my back! Bedridden Li! Can't even get up! Some even thought I might not make it!

Even now, I'm not quite myself still.

Also, if I'd gone - who'd look after my grandson, Abang? He's still at school! And your Pak Soh. Who's going to take care of those two?

---

18 She'll get it!
19 sarong
20 village
21 interior native

Dia orang nakkan Mak Su seorang saja. Mana boleh! Lagi pun nak latihan apa lagi?

Makyong tu kalau masih nak berlatih latih jugak lagi, tak dan lah. Entahlah kalau nak buat Makyong moden. Moden moden tu Mak Su tak mainlah.

Kau Li, gapo mari ke T'ganu ni? Dah lama benar tak jumpa. Dulu masa main di Sental Maket Mak Su tak dapat jumpa Li. Dok talipon talipon Li tapi tak dapat. Entahlah kalau Li ke luar negeri, tak taulah Mak Su.

Apa? Nak intebiew Mak Su? Hai apa pulak nak tebiew tebiew ni. Untuk majalah ke? Mak Su siapalah. Macam tak da orang lain! *(She laughs.)*

Nak tau pasal Makyong. Hah tanyalah apa kau nak tau. Mak Su royak semua kat kau.

(Mak Su lights another cigarette. She settles herself comfortably. She uses her towel to wipe her perspiration. Whatever she does, her gesticulations and her mannerisms cannot hide her bearing as a Makyong prima donna. She is an authentic <u>Seri Panggung</u> and speaks of her art with the casual arrogance of someone who knows.)

Makyong tu memang darah daging Mak Su. Tak boleh cakaplah lagi. Memang seni tu dah sebati benar. Orang kata dah macam isi dengan kuku. Tak boleh dipisahkan lagi. Mak Su tu Makyong. Makyong tu Mak Su. Gitulah.

(Mak Su pours Li a drink, as she continues with her story.)

Jadi masa Mak Su kecik kecik dulu dah tau benar dengan rombongan rombongan Makyong. Mereka selalu datang main di kampung Mak Su.

Mak Su masa kecik dulu memang dah ada suara. Bila Mak Su mengaji Koran orang dah mula puji suara Mak Su. Lemak merdu orang kata. Pandai berlagu.

Tu lah. Bakat ada. Minat pun ada.

(Mak Su lights another cigarette.)

Oi, Mak Su dari mula dulu memang minat Makyong. Bila rombongan Makyong mari, Mak Su lah yang duduk depan sekali. Duk perati apa tingkahlaku orang Makyong tu. Lagu, cara tari mereka Mak Su teliti tenguk. Mak su ikut ikutlah.

Masa tu Mak Su masih lagi belasan tahun. Bila ada peluang Mak Su belajar sama. Lama lama dapat.

Lama lama terlekat dengan rombongan Makyong.

Emak Mak Su tak kisah Mak Su masuk Makyong. Tak ada halangan langsung. Masa dulu orang wayang kita tak di-pandang rendah oleh masyarakat. Bukan macam sekarang!

 main punya main. Jelajah ceruk kampung dari Siam sampai Kedah. Lama lama nama Mak Su pun timbul. Jadi syhur.

18

They told me I can't bring them. How can Li! And come on! What's the fuss about rehearsals!

Ala, Li! As if I still need to rehearse Makyong at my age! Unless you're doing a modern Makyong. If that's what they're doing I can't be bothered. I'm not into those modern stuff*lah*!

And you? Why are you here, in *T'ganu?* [22] It's been so long since we saw you. We didn't even see you when we performed at *Sental Maket,* [23] the other time. Tried to phone you but cannot get. I don't know, maybe you went overseas.

What? You come to interview me? Eh, what's all this interview? For magazine or what? No other people to interview *ke?* Who am I anyway? *(She laughs)*

Oh, want to know about Makyong... Of course you can... Just ask anything you want. I'll tell you everything!

(Mak Su lights another cigarette. She settles herself comfortably. She uses her towel to wipe her perspiration. Whatever she does, her gesticulations and her mannerisms cannot hide her bearing as a Makyong prima donna. She is an authentic Seri Panggung [24] and speaks of her art with the casual arrogance of someone who knows.)

Makyong is my flesh and blood, Li. No point saying more than that. The art has become me. How to separate the nail from the flesh? Impossible*kan?* I am Makyong. And Makyong is me. That's how it is*lah*...

---

22 Trengganu - name of state
23 Central Market, Kuala Lumpur
24 prima donna

15

Bila Mak Su mula main? Li nak Mak Su ceritakan kisah Makyong?

Hai Li. Makyong dulu bukan macam Makyong sekarang. Dulu segar. Le ni tau sajalah - macam hidup segan mati tak mau.

Anak anak Makyong sekarang bersepah sini sana, di kampung entah di ceruk mana pun Mak Su tak tau.

Karang orang endah tak endah Makyong lagi.

Kadang kadang nak main Makyong pun main curi curi. Lebih lebih lagi di Kelantan. Salah di sisi undang undang Islam kononnya. Dengar dengarnya main Wayang Kulit pun salah le ni!

Entahlah. Mak Su ni jahil. Yang Mak Su tau apa yang Mak Su dah buat dari mula. Itulah sebabnya Mak Su pindah ke T'ganu.

Bukan Mak Su seorang. Boleh katakan banyak lagi Makyong yang ada sama dengan Mak Su datang berhijrah ke T'ganu. Kau tenguk saja. Mak Teh kau, Minah Pak Adik, Si Jah Musang Berjanggut, Timah Anak Gajah, - hah semuanya Makyong belaka tu. Semua di T'ganu le ni!

Masa Mak Su dulu, kalau ada kabar angin nak main Makyong saja - hah seminggu tu tak dok cerita lainlah - Makyong sok moh. Itulah masa gemilang Makyong. Orang minat benar dengan Makyong masa tu.

When I start? Oh, you want to know from beginning. My own story of Makyong!

Hai Li. The old Makyong is not what the Makyong is now. In the old days, it was alive. Segar. [25] Now, you yourself can see what it has become - not dead or alive!

Old Makyong Seri Panggung are all over the place - living their drab life in far flung corners of some poor kampung nobody has heard of.

Nowadays people don't really care about us anymore.

At times we even have to perform Makyong on the s[l] Especially in Kelantan. It's against Islam, konon [26]! I'm t[o] it's even wrong to perform Wayang Kulit [27] nowadays!

Just don't know anymore Li. I am ignorant. What I[ ] what I've been doing since the beginning. All these pro[ ] New laws and all that - that's why we've moved to T'[ ]

I'm not the only one, Li! There were so many of us [ ] together to settle here. Let me see. There's your M[ ] Minah Pak Adik, Si Jah Musang Berjanggut, Tim[ah Anak] Gajah. Aaa, they were all formerly Makyong prin[ ] They all in T'ganu now!

I tell you Li, during my time, in the old days, in o[ ] we hear a Makyong performance is coming - f[ ] week our talk will be nothing but Makyong. [ ] moh! [28] Those were the golden days of Makyo[ng.] were really interested in Makyong then.

---

25 fresh
26 it seems
27 Shadow play
28 entirely

(Mak Su pours Li a drink, as she continues with her story.)

So, even when I was a child, I'd know all the Makyong troupes around. They would always come to our village to perform.

When I was young, I already born with a good voice. People praised my voice when I recite the Koran. Melodious, like the sound of a bamboo flute being played, floating in the breeze. Smooth, lilting. They say I know how to carry a melody.

You know*lah* not only was there talent. There was also a genuine interest.

(Mak Su lights another cigarette.)

Oi! Right from the beginning, I was crazy about Makyong. Long before the performance start I'd be the first to sit on the floor, right in front. So that I can see detail of every movement and gesture of the performers. I'd soak in the melody and the way they dance. I would crane my neck to study every aspect of their stylised manners. Later, on my own, I would imitate them!

That time, still in my early teens, too. When there was a chance, I'd study with them. Soon, I know what to do. How to move. How to dance and sing like them. I know all the Makyong stories.

After a while, I got stuck to a Makyong troupe.

No fuss with my family about me joining a Makyong troupe. No objection at all. Those days our society don't look down on Makyong artists. Not like now!

We performed everywhere. Covered every corner of every little village from Siam to Kedah. We performed to whoever

Mak su pun mula rasa yakin. Mak Su buat rombongan sendiri. Mak Su jadi ketua...Itulah masanya Mak Su gunakan nama Mariam Titisan Air Mata. Gitulah nama rombongan Makyong Mak Su.

Siapa beri nama molek tu?

(Mak Su laughs...She settles to tell a long story.)

Cerita nya panjang Li. Tapi sekadar intebiew, macam ni Li...

Ha...Mak Su masa tu memang dah masyhur dengan babak babak sedih. Bila sedih tu, Mak Su entahlah. Bila Mak Su dengar bahasanya saja, mula rasa pilu. Hati Mak Su rasa sedih. Air mata Mak Su keluar gitu. Bercucuran Li! Mak Su sedih sok moh, menangis sok moh. Orang tenguk pun sama sama sedih. Ada juga yang menangis terus.

Juga pulak kadang kadang sebelum Mak Su berangkat main ke satu satu tempat itu, hujan turun sama Li...!

Jadi ada seorang Cikgu kat kampung ni. Kawan kita juga la. Dia lah dok cadangkan Mak Su gunakan nama Mariam Titisan Air Mata tu. Lama lama nama tu pun lekat la! Nama rombongan Mak Su pun masyhur dengan nama tu.

wanted to see us. Soon, they all knew my name. I became famous.

Experience is the teacher Li. So, I became confident of myself. I formed my own troupe. Naturally, I became the leader... That was the time when I used the name *Mariam Titisan Airmata.*: Mariam of the Teardrops. That was how my troupe got its name.

Who gave us that splendid name?

(Mak Su laughs... and settles to tell a long story.)

It's a long story Li. But for the interview, I'll tell you. It's like this.

Ha... Mak Su at that time was famous already. Especially the dramatic roles. I was made for those sad, sorrowful scenes.

Something always happen when the plot calls for sorrowful feelings. A sad mood takes over. I need only to remember the language, the suffering, the sorrow - in fact, even now as I speak... off I can go... I'd give in to the sadness. *Hiba* [29] Li! Inside me, my liver feels itself being shred into pieces. Can't control the tears trickling down my face. Like little streams. I'd cry pitifully. The audience would also feel the same *rasa*[30]. There will always be some who will also cry with me.

Sometimes Li, even before we started a journey, it rained!

So - there was a teacher from our village. A friend*lah*. He was the one, who suggested we use the name "Mariam of the Teardrops". The name stuck, eventually. And my troupe became famous with that name*lah!*

---

29 grief
30 feeling, sentiment

21

Mak Su ketua kan...

Hoi, susah Li. Makyong tu susah. Tapi susah susah, 'angin' kita segar. Maklumlah dapat kepuasan. Bila dapat main Li, bila orang ramai mari, nama kita naik, senang hati!

Kalau sikit dapat duit pun tak pedulilah. Lepas angin Li! Angin kita sihat! Kita bahagia!

Hah bila Makyong berangkat main Li, bukan sehari dua! Bukan seminggu dua! Kadang kadang sebulan dua! Besar angkatan Makyong kita dulu!

Maklumlah, telebesyen mana ada. Tak macam sekarang! Dulu Makyong segar Li! Suka!

Hah, bila nak berangkat, si tokeh tu siapkanlah lori. Bawalah semua perkakas perkakas - dari papan beloti, periuk belanga, dapur, atap atap zing, peti peti isi pakaian, alat alat musik, bak kata habis semualah keperluan wayang, keperluan hidup sehari, semua di bawa!

Lori tu kalau tak sarat tak jalan lagi! Kadang kadang sampai barang barang nak melempah keluar.

(By this time, Mak Su has settled herself comfortably. It is a hot day. She fans herself.)

I was the leader, you see...

Hoi, Makyong was difficult Li! So difficult. Those were challenging days. But in spite of the suffering, the hard work, we were in high spirits.

Of course - because we're doing what we wanted to do! When we give life to our art, the audience were responsive*lah*. We could be proud of our good name. Worth the effort!

Even if there was little money, we didn't care. Our *angin* [31] was released. Refreshed. We're happy!

When we started on a tour - it wasn't for one or two days. A week or two. Sometimes a whole month or even two! It was a big troupe then, Li!

Of course, there was no television those days. Not like now. At that time, Makyong was very popular and in great form! Those were wonderful times!

Hah, when we'd decided to go, the manager would hire a lorry to take our things. And my God, did we take everything! - beams, planks, pots and pans, stoves, zinc roofing, boxes of costumes, musical instruments - the lot! I mean, just about everything we wanted to use on stage and our everyday needs away from home.

The lorry was jam-packed, Li! Why, it wouldn't be allowed to move otherwise. Sometimes things seemed about to spill out. Burst out of the lorry's sides!

(By this time, Mak Su has settled herself comfortably. It is a hot day. She fans herself.)

---

31 vital force

Apa Li? Kau nak tau kehidupan kita sehari hari? Eh kalau ia pun - ye la... Sabarlah sikit. Hai orang Kelumpur ni. Semua nak ekpress! Mana boleh?

Hah ye la! Kalau sampai tempat main tu, maklumlah, anak Makyong mestilah tau jaga nama.

Orang b'tina Li, selalunya duduk dalam panggung. Jarang keluar siang hari. Hai hilang seri nanti. Kita main bertiket kan. Lain lah macam sekarang - untuk toris.

Nak mandi, nak berak - dia orang Makyong tu pandai Li. Malam baru keluar.

Yang keluar siang beli barang barang - beras, sayur, ikan semua nya orang lakilah! Yang ada suami tu, suamilah pegi!

Hah mestilah. Suami mestilah ikut sama! Kalau tidak Makyong tu tak mainlah Li!

(Mak Su chain smokes.)

Hah, orang b'tina, malam baru keluar. Dah mandi, bersih siap, make-uplah.

Bedak make-up gapo pakai?

What Li? You want to know how we live our everyday life? Eh even so, can't you let me have my breath back! Oh you people from *Kelumpur!* Everything you want fast. Express. Impossible - you city folk!

Hah ye la! When we got to our destination, we must live up to our good name. No messing around!

The women folk will stay in our make-shift theatre compound. Seldom allowed to go out during the day. Well, we'll lose our glow otherwise. *Hilang seri!* [32] People pay to see us, Li! Not free like now. It's not the same when you perform for tourists.

The women only came out at night - to bathe or go to toilet. The Makyong women were clever, Li. Things were trained to come out only at night!

Now, who will go out during the daytime? To buy rice, vegetable, fish and the rest of the food? Menfolk, of course! If you're married, your husband*lah* will go!

Of course! Husbands must come along! If not, there won't be any performance!

(Mak Su chain smokes)

Hah, us womenfolk would only come out at night. When we've finished our bath and our toilet - we'd start our make-up*lah!*

What sort of make-up we use?

---

32 lose special glow

Eh, e-eh make-up pancake gapo namanya?

Bedak Mek Fekter! Oi, Mahal Li! Masa mula Mak Su pakai tu - tiga rial. Kemudian empat, lima, enam - hah sampai naik dua belas!

Mak Su tak boleh pakai bedak lain. Naik jerawat - punah muka!

Makeup, dua tiga puluh sekali beli Li!

Mak Su dulu Li, lawa selalu! Kalau tak main pun, podar gincu mesti ada. Tak macam sekarang. Dulu jangan! Kalau tak main wayang pun mesti lawa selalu! Kalau tidak, tak sedap.

Kita orang mainan kan... Bukan cara orang kampung. Orang kampung podar seminggu sekali tak sentuh muka pun tak apa! Kita orang wayang tak boleh...

Hah kalau dah pakai makeup tu, bukanlah Mak Su nak puji, kalau orang tenguk - lain! Siang lain, malam lain, Li!

Kalau masa main, dah make-up, pakai Pakyong - bukanlah Mak Su nak puji diri, macam orang umur dua puluh lapan tahun! Berseri!

Ye lah. Bukan bedak saja. Adalah syarat syarat pakai bedak tu. Adalah baca bacaan untuk menyerikan muka. Li tak kan tak tau!

Oh yes, it's *Mek Fekter!* [33] Oi, it wasn't cheap! When I first used it, it was only three ringgit. Then it went to four, five, six - and rose even to twelve, Li!

Couldn't use any other brand. I'd break out in pimples. Ruined my face.

Li, it was nothing spending twenty, thirty ringgit on make-up.

In those days, I was always made-up. Even when I wasn't performing, powder and lipstick were a must. Not like now. Those days even when we're not on stage we'd make sure that we looked good. Just doesn't seem right if we didn't!

We are artists...Li. Not village peasants. Doesn't matter if for a week they don't put powder on their face. But when you are an artist, it doesn't seem right somehow...

Now Li, when I'm all made-up - not that I'm praising myself - heads turned. Something happens - I'd look different. During the day, I'd look different. By night, I'm again another person!

During a performance, after being fully made-up and in my *Pakyong* [34] costume. I'm not exaggerating, Li - I'd look twenty-eight!

Berseri! [35] I'd be radiant!

Of course - it's not just the powder. There're other things you must do on top of that! There are *jampi* [36] you must recite to make your face more beautiful. As if you don't know about all this...

---

33 Max Factor
34 Makyong hero
35 glowing
36 incantations

27

Li tak dok ayat ayat untuk menyerikan muka?

Heh apa malu malu cakap. Nanti Mak Su ajarkan jampi jampi untuk baca.

Kita orang mainan Li! Mesti pandai jaga muka, badan. Gerak geri gaya kita mesti menawan. Kan kita main bertiket. Kita orang wayang mesti lawa selalu!

Mak Su kalau dah makeup. Sikat rambut. Kalau dah pakai Pakyong. Suaru merdu... Cara gerak geri kita menawan. Kita bukan lagi orang biasa. Kita raja. Kita orang kayangan. Kita ada sakti!

Ah Li! Bila Mak Su dah pakai Pakyong, pakaian jantan tu - sampai ada orang b'tina tergila gilakan Mak Su.

Dia kata dia balik tak boleh tidur. Dengar dalam telinga suara Mak Su. Duk terdengar dengar. Duk ternampak nampak. Duk tak makan minum Li!

B'tina sama b'tina. Nak buat gapo, Li!

Hai Li! Kalau nak cerita - panjang Li! Panjang!

Cerita cerita di balik tabir Makyong!

(Mak Su laughs nostalgically.)

Hai, ada pulak yang iri hati, hasat dengki bila nama kita masyhur. Ada pulak orang yang membuat pitenah untuk menjatuhkan nama baik kita. Sebab itulah kita mesti hati hati, pandai jaga diri dari niat jahat orang.

Really you don't?

Don't be shy about it. It's no secret in the theatre. Everybody uses it. I'll teach you a special *jampi* that's really effective.

We're stage artists, Li! We must look after our face. Our body. Our manners. The way we carry ourselves must be attractive. People pay to see us. We performers must always look good!

When I've put on my make-up. My hair in place. And wearing my *Pakyong* costume. My voice lilting, melodious... Moving with such grace. We're no longer ordinary people. We're kings. *Dewas*. [37] We radiate magic!

Ah Li! When I become the hero - in my *Pakyong* costume, there are times when even the women would go crazy about me! I remember there was one woman who said she couldn't sleep when she got back home. Kept hearing my voice. Again and again Li. In her ears. Kept seeing me everywhere. Then she lost appetite for food or drink!

Woman and woman! Can you imagine Li? What can they do?

Hai Li! If I tell you everything - it'll take all day.

Those funny stories behind the stage curtain.

(Mak Su laughs nostalgically.)

There were also those who were envious and green with jealousy when your name starts to get popular. And there're always those who'd start rumours or libel you to bring down

---

37 Gods

Hai, orang Li! Nak buat gapo!

Tak boleh ceritalah. Ni semua pekara biasa di panggung. Mesti jugak ada politiknya.

(Mak Su hears something. It's her grandson 'Abang' who has just returned from school.)

Hah, tu dia si Abang baru balik dari sekolah.

Abang! Mai sini. Mai jumpa dengan Bang Li kau dari Kelumpur ni.

Pergi salam! Abang bukan main suka dengan beg yang Li belikan dia masa Kelumpur dulu. Hai budak budak sekarang, kecik kecik lagi dah tau nak lawa Li... Minum lagi Li. Mak Su ambilkan lagi Teh.

(Mak Su goes to the kitchen. Abang, Mak Su's grandson switches on the Radio. An R.Azmi song is broadcast Mak Su returns with a fresh pot of tea.)

Eh, budak ni... Kuat sangat radio tu Bang!

(Mak Su however is affected by the infectious rhythm of the song. As she helps her guest with the tea she starts to enjoy the R.Azmi song.)

your good name. That's why you must be careful to guard yourself against these evil intentions.

Hai, people will be people, Li!

No need for me to say more*lah!* These are normal everyday things in the theatre. There will always be the politics.

(Mak Su hears something. It's her grandson 'Abang' who has just returned from school.)

Hah, here he is! Abang's back from school.

Abang! ABANG! Come over here. Come and meet your Brother Li, from *Kelumpur.*

Go on! Give him your greetings! Abang loves the bag you bought him the other day he was in *Kelumpur.* Hai, kids nowadays. So vain already at such a young age! Heh, have more drink Li.

Tea's finished. I'll get some more...

(Mak Su goes to the kitchen. Abang, Mak Su's grandson switches on the radio. An R.Azmi song is broadcast. Mak Su returns with a fresh pot of tea.)

Eh, this boy is too much... The radio is too loud, Bang!

(Mak Su however is affected by the infectious rhythm of the song. As she helps her guest with the tea she starts to enjoy, and dance to the R.Azmi song.)

Mak Su dulu semua boleh belaka Li! Bukan Makyong saja. Bukan Nora saja. Joget, dansing dansing orang puteh tu semua boleh Mak Su buat.

(Mak Su 'shows off' a rumba to the R.Azmi song. She stops when she has had enough.)

Heh, tutup radio tu Bang! *(She settles down again).*

Hai, kita orang wayang Li. Kadang kadang ada jugak kita di undang buat joget. Masa suka suka. Taulah kalau ada keramaian, sambutan orang kenamaan, tukar orang besar. Masa suka ria. Jogetlah.

Joget orang putih - Wolz, Selow Fok, Tengo, Cha Cha tu semua Mak Su buat dulu. Bukanlah selalu!

Mak Su masa muda dulu semua tu Mak Su teray!

Kalau dah pandai Makyong, Tengo, Cha Cha tu apa susahnya Li!

(Mak Su lights another cigarette and at the same time fans herself. She reminisces...)

Susah Li. Makyong ni susah.

Makyong ni tak boleh nak belajar cepat cepat. Tak boleh nak buat cepat cepat.

In the old days Li, I could do ANY dance. Not just Makyong. Not just *Nora* [38] I could also do the *joget* [39] and all the *joget orang putih.* [40]

(Mak Su 'shows off' a rumba to the R.Azmi song. She stops when she has had enough.)

Heh, switch off the radio, Bang! *(She settles down again.)*

Hai, we're performers through and through Li! Sometimes we would be invited to do the *joget.* When there was a celebration. You know - when there is a gathering, perhaps to receive a VIP, or when a high official goes on a transfer. Time for a party. *Temasya.* [41] Time to *jogetlah!*

Joget orang putih - wols, slow fok, tengo, cha-cha [42] - used to dance them at one time. But not often*lah.*

When I was young, I tried everything!

A la! If you've already mastered Makyong - what's so difficult about *tengo, cha-cha,* Li!

(Mak Su lights another cigarette and at the same time fans herself. She reminisces...)

It's difficult. Difficult Li. Makyong is not easy.

Can't learn Makyong quickly. You can't dance it quickly either.

---

38 Menora - a Kelantan-Siamese genre of dance-drama
39 popular folk-dance
40 white man's dances
41 festive occasion
42 waltz, slow fox, tango, cha-cha

Mesti tau nyanyi. Ada tari. Ada lawak. Kalau tidak tak cukup syarat. Angin tak lepas.

Itulah dia nasib Makyong ni. Tak main, tak doh pitih. Kalau main. Nak ada angin.

Kalau Mak Su main, mesti nak ada angin. Bukan Mak Su bila main, nak duit saja - Tidak Li!

Bila kita main tak dok angin, kita tak boleh tenguk penonton. Kita malu.

Kita sepatutnya lebih dari orang yang menengok kita. Jadi kita tak malulah.

Masa Mak Su maju, masa muda dulu, Mak Su ada upaya.

Kalau Mak Su rasa penonton mencabar, kalau penonton mintak kita sejengkal, Mak Su boleh beri mereka dua jengkal.

Mak Su ada kekuatan luar biasa. Boleh memberi kuasa pada gerak geri gaya Mak Su.

Kalau Mak Su jadi emak, jadi emak
Kalau jadi jantan, jadi jantan
Kalau jadi budak, jadi budak...
Tempat sedih, sedih
Tempat bengkeng, bengkeng.

Boleh katakan Mak Su sendiri boleh kontrol suasana panggung tu!

(Light slowly dims.)

34

Not only you must know the song, there is also the dance which you must master. Then there is the comedy. If not, Makyong is not complete. No *angin*.

I guess that's the fate of Makyong. If you don't perform - there is no money. And when you perform it you must be in the right mood. The right *angin*.

When I perform the Makyong, I must have the *angin*. I don't perform just for money. Oh no!

When we don't have the *angin*, we can't look the audience in the eye. We'd be embarrassed!

We should be above the audience! Then only no room for *malu*.[43] No time to be awkward on stage Li! Means you're not ready!

In my heyday, when I was young. I had that power.

Whenever the audience challenged me - I could rise to the challenge. I could give them double what they asked for!

I had such extraordinary power. I'd ooze inner strength in all my gestures.

I could be a mother, when the part requires it...
Or convincing enough as a man.
When I am child, I feel and behave like one.
When sad, I'd grieve...
But when angry, watch out - I can be frighteningly so...

You can say I alone could control the mood in that theatre!

(Light slowly dims.)

---

43 shyness

Sekarang lain Li. Mak Su dah tua. Lumpuh peringatan. Lupa! lama tak buat, lupalah. Siapa tak lupa!

Sekarang nak main Makyong pun susah. Semua nak cepat. Orang lekas bosan. Apa tak bosan - sekarang orang tak tahu cerita. Tak tau lagu. Tak macam orang dulu. Orang sekarang lebih suka tenguk telebesyen.

Di Kelantan lagi teruk. Lain sakit nya.

Serupa orang kata dah jatuh ditimpa tangga. Itulah nasib Makyong sekarang. Entahlah bila Mak Su mati nanti, Makyong nampaknya mati sama...

Makyong cerita moden? Cerita baru?

Hai, Makyong tu cerita tawarikh Li! Cerita Raja Raja. Cerita Istana. Raja Gondang. Dewa Muda. Petri Timun Muda. Anak Raja Tangkai Hati. Banyak ceritanya. Mak Su tak bolehlah nak royak. Banyak dah lupa.

Dalam cerita, dalam lagu makyong tu kita boleh tau keadaan hidup Raja Raja dulu.

Misal nya, sambil menyanyi Mak Su bilang macam mana Raja pakai baju, sarung seluar, kain lilit pinggang, pakai selendang, taruh tanjak - ini semua Mak Su sebut dalam nyanyi menghadap rebab!

Now it's different. I'm old. My memory is poor. I forget many lines. Forgotten! Of course I've forgotten them!

Well! If you don't do things often enough, if you only perform once or twice a year - naturally you start to be out of practice. You get rusty. You forget your songs. You would too! Any artist needs to perform always Li!

Nowadays you can't even perform the real Makyong. Or everything has to be done quickly. People get bored easily. Of course, they'd get bored! Nowadays, nobody knows the story. Not familiar with the melodies. Not like the old days. Nowadays everybody prefers television.

In Kelantan, it's worse. There, it's a different problem!

Like the old saying. Not only you've fallen - but the ladder's also crashed on you... That's the fate of Makyong now. Don't know. When I die, I guess Makyong will die with me...

Modern Makyong? With modern stories?

Hai, Makyong's about our past, Li! Stories of our rajas. Their olden courts. *Raja Gondang, Dewa Muda, Petri Timun Muda Anak Raja Tangkai Hati.*[44] Oh, lots more. Can't tell off hand. There're lots more I've forgotten.

From the Makyong story, from the songs, we can learn about the ways of our ancient ancestors. Our ancient courts.

For instance, when I sing, I would describe how the *raja* would put on his regalia - from his *baju,* [42] his trousers, the long cummerbund around his waist, his sash, his traditional

---

44 Names of old Makyong stories
45 jacket

Buat apa disebut gitu?

MASA DIA GITU!
Pakaian raja! Cerita Istana! Zaman dulu! Zaman Makyong dulu!

(Mak Su recites part of the Menghadap Rebab, demonstrating using solely her selendang, the various gestures of preparation of a Raja that is the essence of this ritualised beginning of a Makyong performance.)

Ambil seluar sauh kekaki gak
Baju kami duk time, time ke badan
Kalu kain selendang gak jantan
Ambil keris sisik mengiring
Kain belit di pinggang
Tiga belit bertemu gak pucur
Ambil La sangkut ke bahu
Tanjak kami duk tenggek, tenggek ke dahi.

Makyong tu PESAKA Li!

(Mak Su sighs. She is almost exhausted. Suddenly there is thunder and lightning. The hot afternoon has brought a brief thunderstorm.)

Hai, panas sangat tadi! Sekarang hujan pulak. Untung Si Abang ada tolong bawak sotong masuk.

headgear - all this I'd recite in the song called *Menghadap Rebab.* [46]

Why do I recite these things?

Eh, Makyong is about that time Li!
It is about our ancestors, our rajas, the court days, ancient times! Makyong times!

(Mak Su recites part of the <u>Menghadap Rebab</u>, demonstrating solely with her <u>selendang</u> [47] the various gestures in the preparation of a raja, a characteristic ritualised beginning of a Makyong performance.)

As the trousers fold up the legs
And the shirt covers the torso
The *selendang* of a special kind
The kris adorns the side
The cummerbund, the waist around
Three times meeting at the seam
The shoulder, a cloth hangs on
Head-dress is placed, rightly, above the forehead...

Makyong is our heritage Li!

(Mak Su sighs. She is almost exhausted. Suddenly there is a clap of thunder and lightning. The hot afternoon has brought a brief thunderstorm.)

Fine and hot a minute ago! Now it's raining. Strange weather... Luckily, Abang helped bring in the *sotong*.

---

46 'facing the Rebab' - Malay spiked fiddle
47 shawl

Memang dah lama tak hujan! Hujan pun sikit sikit Li. Bukan hujan betul betul! Kat Kelumpur selalu hujan dengarnya! Itulah rahmat tuhan! Hujan - Titisan Airmata Makyong.

Apa kau kata Li? Kau ada tape Mak Su buat Makyong di rumah kau dulu? Eh, beri Mak Su nak dengar!

(Mak Su takes a cassette tape. She puts it in the player. As she listens, Mak Su is emotionally moved. The recording is of an episode that she particularly adores... a sad scene in a Makyong performance. Mak Su gesticulating with the recording, slowly getting up. She has forgotten her guest. Alone in her own world, she starts to walk about, the walk becoming a stylised Makyong gait. She is reliving her performance in her mind.)

(Music changes to an evocative chant inspired by a Makyong tune. The melodious chant brings out the various rasas of Mak Su - a longing of the past, of days when she was able to soar with her art. The lights slowly fade out on Mak Su.)

Tamat

It's true. Hasn't rained here for some time now. Even when it rains, it's just few drops. Nothing serious. I heard that it rains often in *Kelumpur*, Li. Well, - God's gift! Rain. It always reminds me of the teardrops of Makyong.

What did you say Li? You have a tape? My performance the other day at your place? Eh, I'd love to hear it. Come, come give it to me!

(Mak Su takes a cassette tape. She puts it in the player. As she listens, Mak Su is emotionally moved. The recording is of an episode that she particularly adores... a sad scene in a Makyong performance. Mak Su gesticulates with the recording, slowly getting up. She has forgotten her guest. Alone in her own world, she starts to walk about, the walk becoming a stylised Makyong gait. She is reliving her performance in her mind.)

(Music changes to an evocative chant inspired by a Makyong tune. The melodious chant brings out the various rasas of Mak Su - a longing for the past, of days when she was able to soar with her art. The lights slowly fade out on Mak Su.)

End

SECOND FLUSH

SARASA
The Dance-Mother

Sabera Shaik as Sarasa

Brief Notes on the Character:

Sarasa is a woman in her early fifties, married to Siva, an unassuming man who apparently cannot be bothered arguing with his nagging wife and usually lets her have the final say in all household matters.

They have three children, two elder boys - Anand and Sankar - who are now old enough to earn their own keep, and a daughter Komala, a vivacious eighteen year-old of considerable artistic talent.

Sarasa is a thinnish, dowdy and unimpressive woman with a rodent-like face and mannerisms. She is impatient and seems nervous most of the time. She can't sit still for long and is always fidgeting and looking around her with sharp, glittering eyes for something to do.

She gushes, stammers and speaks in a whining kind of manner. She is basically a housewife with unfulfilled matriarchal pretensions. She is a gossip and busybody but, being rather simple, one sees through her cunning and deviousness straight away. Sarasa is cunning and devious for one reason only - her daughter, Komala. She is ambitious for her daughter and sees her self-appointed role in stage-managing her daughter's dancing and stage career as part of her own destiny. Sarasa is almost a chronic case of a mother who is besotted with her daughter. At the same time Sarasa casts herself as the used and forsaken heroine typically found in the Hindi or Tamil melodramas which have been an integral part of her exposure to and understanding of life.

Since young, Sarasa has been infatuated and caught up with the trappings of tinsel and glamour of the type of theatre found in local drama, variety shows and temple gatherings. For a particular segment of Indian housewives in a relatively busy city like Kuala Lumpur, these and Indian cinema videos have been reference points for her sentiments and made indelibly strong impressions. For Sarasa they signify the high points of her life.

Since Komala was born, Sarasa has smothered her with a rather intense kind of love and possessiveness, showered her with expensive girlish gifts, from tarty dresses to showy jewellery. At the same time she was passionately strict disciplinarian with the child, obsessed that Komala should be the best in whatever she does - especially in her Terpsichorean endeavours.

In an endless string of private dance, music and singing classes, Sarasa insists on being present to personally take notes and supervise each correction much to the exasperation and chagrin of the teachers. As much as she thinks she is doing the right thing (often due to her own lack of exposure, education and understanding of the art beyond what she has absorbed from watching endless cinema films and amateur productions), Sarasa's advice is addressed to the adolescent daydreams that fill the vacuum in her own life. In no small measure has she reminded everybody, especially Komala, of the sacrifice and hard work that she herself has unselfishly and unstintingly invested in her dedication to her daughter.

Sarasa has of course not been aware of the undercurrent of dissatisfaction and rebellion raging in her young daughter. She finds it incomprehensible that her daughter could have run off with the tailor's son and remains convinced that other people are to blame for poisoning her daughter's mind and plotting against her, unable to come to terms with the reality that she is now faced with.

SARASA

Prelude Music:
Indian Film Music - the cheap and common variety

Scene:
Komala's bedroom.

The whole of this scene is reminiscent of an Indian movie sequel. With exaggerated melodrama, breast beating, hair pulling and wailing.
Sarasa has just found out that her daughter Komala has eloped with the local tailor's son - the son of her worst enemy.
Sarasa is losing her head. She storms into the emptiness of her daughter's room. She rummages aimlessly through the wardrobe and drawers... She speaks in pidgin, ungrammatical and colloquial Malaysian-English.
Sarasa is wearing a plain sari. Her hair is short, rather dowdy. She had a few months ago shaven her hair at Batu Caves to propitiate a vow made for Komala and the hair is just growing back.

Gone! Everyting gone! Finish!

What people will tink? My daughter!

Eeiii! Kadavale! What have I done to deserve this punishment? I have done my vows. I've carried my kavadi up Batu Caves. I've given you your presents. Then, why all dis mess? Why dis fate? Must I lose face? My face is now mud! Why? Why? Why? *(She sobs)*

My life's finished. What people will tink now?

Dey will laugh. Oh I know dey will laugh behind my back. Dey are just waiting for someting like dis to happen. They pray for my downfall.

I will kill myself. Den dey'll be sorry. But first I will kill the boy. No, I will kill the pariah fader first.

Komala! To run away with a common tailor's son. My Number One enemy! I am sure dat rotten Ravi knew dis all along.

He must've encouraged his son to spite me! What he got to lose? He's a man!

And Komala my jewel! How can you do dis? How can you do dis to your darling Amma? I told you many times. Don't trust any man. Not even your own fader.

You don't listen to your Amma. Now everyting is messy. My darling daughter. My Lakshmi. My lotus bud. My Saraswati.

SIVA!

Siva! Siva! Siva! You useless husband!

Siva! Your fault. All your fault. Useless fader!

Always never home! Always work! Work! Office! Meeting!

I'm just a woman! All alone to run dis big house. I go to market. I wash. I cook. I bring up childrun. Send to school. Send to class. All problems I am solving. I am scolding everybody. Fight everybody. De dance teachers. Music teachers. Parents. Tailors. Even judges!

Komala, how I fought for you - hands and teeth. Remember de Dance Competition? You danced so gorgeously and dey

put you Number Two. Dat Bhavani girl got first. But I didn't
let dem. I fought de verdict.

They put you Number Two! Number Two! Who are dey?
Dose stupid judges. You are always de best. Always first.
Never Number Two...

How you dance. How beautifool your *abhinaya*. Your sweet
smile. Yes always smiling when you dance. Smile Komala, I
always tell you. Smile! SMILE! You must always smile when
you dance.

So quick time I marched to the judges. I told dem what I
think.

Who are you? I asked dem. What you know about dance?
What your qualify? I told dem off. You are all corrupt! Taken
bribe from parents! All of you! My daughter never get second.
Never! Never! Never! She's first class dancer. Over my dead
body - I showed dem my slippers.

I will pull out! I will go to the newspaper! I make big protest!

I tretened dem. Der was big, big scene.

Dey got frightened. All the judges. Dey were housewives anyway. Dey got frightened and den dey changed deir mind and
gave you first place.

Yes, people are jealous! Dey are jealous because deir daughter
can never match you. I have de most talented daughter in the
world!

No one can beat you Komala.

I am not caring what people will say. When you come back, I
will show them all...

O Komala, you are everyting to me. My little Lakshmi. My lotus bud. My Saraswati. Where is my baby?

(Sarasa limps to the wardrobe. It is filled with an array of gaudy dance costumes, hairpieces and bells. There is a dancing doll dressed in an Indian dance costume. She lovingly takes out, a good sample of the costumes, spreads and admires them and inspects the array of costumes and jewellery. She puts the doll in the centre. The following monologue is addressed to the doll whom she visualises as Komala.)

Each of your costume has a story to tell. Each jewellery reminds me of someting.

I keep everyting. Since you were small baby. Precious memories. As mader, I alone know.

How lovingly I used to tie your hair, put your flowers, your jewelleries. Den your sari-costume.

Yes, before you dance, you look like a goddess. No one can beat your beauty. Oh, you were so, so gorgeous.

(She remembers other beautiful costumes and goes to the wardrobe to take more out. She prances in a gawky dance walk and poses with the costumes. She spreads them all over the floor. She then sees a particular costume. She screams with rage. She throws it out. She almost froths at the mouth with venomous hate.)

Rascal! I hate you. Ravi! - I hope you come back as a dog in your next life. I will get my revenge on you, Ravi!

Even after I die, I will follow you. I will torture you. My ghost will spit on your face forty times everyday.

My ghost will follow you and make your life miserable...
I...I...will... *(She breaks down again.)*

I never like those costumes you sow my daughter, anyway!
(She wails, in defeat.)

(Spoken in a soft wailing kind of voice, Sarasa pours out her inner feelings.)

My daughter, she is all I got. She is everyting to me. I live for her... My other two sons can do anything dey want. I don't care. Dey are men - dey will always survive, anyhow. Besides they will all marry one day. Den dey leave de house, dey have family - I no place: noting in deir lives. Wat I do when I'm old with them. De wife will choose her mader to look after her childrun.

Not with my Komala. She must come back. Then I will find her de right husband. She will let me look after de house. Look after de babies. I will have a place when I am old.

Daughters always look after you when you are old. I see dis happening to ader women.

And Komala, so talented. So beautiful. She will surely find a rich husband. Good husband.

But she is still young. First I want her to be famous. She must dance first. She must be on stage. Dance! Do everyting I no chance to do.

Perhaps later be famous like a film star.

I plan to go to India. After her Form Six. Soon.

I will take her with me. She will dance in Madras. I've saved enough money. Only God knows what sacrifice I go through, to save for that child. Look at me! Do you see a nice sari for myself?

Yes, I will take her to Madras. She will dance dere.
Someone will surely notice her.
Who knows, perhaps a movie director!

I will tell Komala what to do. We women know how to handle dose men. We know what dey want...

I will teach Komala how to be sexy. How to get attention. How to get roles.

Den she will really start a career. She will go up and up. Dere will be no stopping.

Of course, she will act. That is easy. Komala can laugh, she can cry, or be angry - so beautifully. You want to laugh, cry or be angry with her. She will have no problem dancing in de film.

Those sad, sad film will be perfect for her.

I will be by her side. Every minute, every hour and day. She will surely need her Amma.

(Sarasa picks up the costumes that she had flung in anger at the same time mumbling about looking after her daughter.)

I will look after your food, make sure you have your hot drinks, I will be by your side every minute, you need your Amma to look after you, I will make you a champion dancer....

(And suddenly, as if she remembers another strategy that could help her stage-manage Komala's career...)

Or she can always start a dance school. Now every girl wants to dance. And every dancer wants to open a dance school.

But Komala is not just any dancer. Everyone knows dat.

She has everybody's high opinion. With her name surely every girl will want to dance like her.

Girls will want her to teach dem. Dey will all come to her for training. Dere will be more and more students.

De school will grow big. And famous.

We can have our own shows. Our own dance dramas. Own musicians. Komala will curry...currygraph.

Of course, she will take de main role. She will have many, many maids. Sakis! Dere will be many, many beautiful costume changes.

Dere will be dry-ice effects. Smoke. Colourful lights. Beautiful glittering costumes, jewelleries. Fine head-dresses. Maybe fireworks! Oh, I can see it. It will be SO gorgeous!

Of course. With my experience, I can guide her. I've watched how de other teachers do it. I've even taken notes. I know all the contacts - the musicians, tailors, lighting man - everyting. I have their addresses and phone numbers. Definitely Komala will need my help.

Dose parents have to be controlled. Especially de parents. I know how to handle them. Dose parents are very bad. All dey tink of are deir daughters. So selfish!

But some of the teachers are too much. Too proud! And jealous!

53

How can dey not let me sit in class. And dey won't let Komala learn from other teachers. How can dey stop Komala from learning everyting. Dey can't teach everyting? Dey are not like the Gurus from India! Dey are just local teachers!

Now Komala has learnt everyting! I make sure dat! She has learnt all items! And she's done her *arangetram*! So gorgeous performance. Pah! she doesn't need these local teachers anymore!

Of course, I shall be very, very strict when Komala has her own school. No one but Komala and me should be in class.

No one in make-up room during performance, too! They will all do what I say because, if not, their daughters will be expelled! Out! I say!

Oh yes, I know those Indian minds.

Dey will take everyting from you and den leave. Dey are jealous and dey want to be more famous den Komala. But I will tell Komala not to teach everyting. It's dangerous to teach everyting. Why! Dey will take everyting, dey will steal your music, your students, your ideas - even your costumes! Den dey leave you - with noting! I know. I've seen dis happen...

Oh no! You must never teach them everyting. You must keep some so dat dey will come back for more!!! You must know how to handle dese terrible people.

The maders are de worst!

(Sarasa returns to her costumes and jewelleries...and the doll)

Yes, I will protect my baby! You will be famous...

You can do everyting I had no chance to do.

I used to watch the stars when they act, when dey dance.
I only get small parts. Maids' parts. Sakis' parts...

(Sarasa once again plays with the costumes. She examines a roll of artificial paper flowers belonging to her daughter. She puts them in her hair. She puts on a tiara. A pair of gaudy earrings. A golden, sequined shawl. She is looking at herself in the mirror...She puts lipstick and rouge on her face...)

So pretty! So gorgeous! I can dress you up everytime you perform... I love to do that...

You look like de Goddess Laksmi...

Everyting I cannot do... wanted to do...

Music Special: A typical Bombay Film song. Sarasa does a cheap vulgar dance that one sees all the time in those films. A sort of a striptease around the banana trees.

Then suddenly the Villain appears - predictably in the form of Ravi, the tailor, whom she hates. A rape scene - done in the most melodramatic overacting - just like in the movies...

She comes out, once again dishevelled, beaten, raped in the melodrama of her own making... Looking at the audience, in the way Indian film actresses do, biting the end of her shawl, staring into the middle distance, crying...holding the doll.

Komala... Komala... Komala...

Slow fade out of lights.

End

THIRD FLUSH

DEENA
The Food Lover

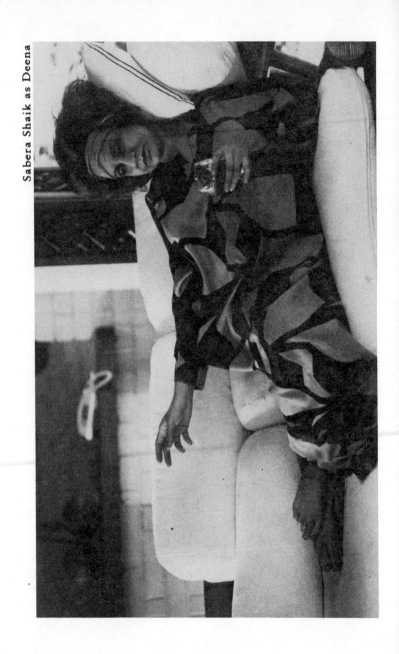

Sabera Shaik as Deena

Background Notes

Deena is a woman in her sixties. She is rather on the 'large' side, and one can still see the remains of a singular beauty.

She is one of those Eurasians of rather obscure pedigree - could be of mixed Anglo-Indian-Parsi antecedents - that somehow one associates with the colonial era.

Though large, she somehow carries her weight well, and is obviously relatively well-to-do, widely travelled, and broad-minded in her outlook.

She is well-integrated with the 'Malayan' society and knows the culture well.

Deena's main preoccupation in life is her love for food; a love she cultivated with slow relish from the time her beloved husband, Colonel James MacIntosh was murdered.

Having lost her husband (her first and only love) in a tragic and macabre ambush by the communists during the early Emergency days, she has lived alone since her two children left to set up their own lives. The family home is a comfortable colonial house.

Through her husband's postings, the family was on the move most of the time, and it was during this period that she got to know and grew fond of the cosmopolitan Malayan way of life and culture. She learnt to speak Malay and even a smattering of Cantonese and decided to stay a while in Malaya after the Colonel's tragic death, at least till the children could go to college. In former times she had hobnobbed with the higher echelons of the Malay aristocracy, British commissioners as well as the wives of the Malay policemen and the Chinese vegetable-sellers in the local market. One expects her now to be in the company of upper class socialite circles known for their cosmopolitan tastes and patronage of the arts.

The shock of her husband's death, which left a part of her devastated and desolate, was a turning point in her life; symbolised by two traits: she began to be obsessed with food, and took to the habit of smoking cigars - of course, her husband's brand.

Whenever her thoughts linger on her beloved and departed husband, Deena involuntarily craves for something to eat, and when the memory of her lost marital bliss comes to her mind, she will be found staring vacantly into the middle distance with moist eyes, her hand groping to light the nearest cigar, regardless of where she is.

Despite a wide circle of friends, no other companion has replaced her husband. Deena is kept busy enough with invitations, and her own soirées are meeting grounds for an assortment of poets, painters and performers of sorts. However, typically, Deena is ultimately on her own and used to keeping her own company, glued to the TV, playing solitary card games or holding conversations with herself that allow free rein to her opinions and reminiscences.

Certainly one could say that as time passed and as Deena gradually graduated from being nicely plump to a rather large lady of considerable presence, her reputation as an immaculate food connoisseur also increased.

She herself had always been a wonderful cook, and had always preferred to do her own cooking, even when there were amahs in residence. It was in cooking that she was able to find herself in a world where she was both mistress and magician.

DEENA

Prelude Music:
Keroncong music.

Scene:
A living-room parlor.

Deena, wearing a comfortably loose kaftan, reclining on a chaise-lounge or 'planters' lazy chair, her left hand deftly operating a TV remote control, and the right mechanically but daintily picking on an assortment of nuts, chocolates, petits fours, glazed food, etc. She wears a pair of thick but fashionable glasses.

The time is approximately 3.00 pm. She is supposed to be having her siesta but is apparently not able to... Deena switches on the TV.

What rubbish they show nowadays. Don't they have anything better than badminton tournaments, pop shows, *Drama Minggu Ini?* And of course, we have to pay for our middle-class sins.

(Advertisement for Pizza fast food...)

Advertising!

There's just nothing interesting!

Never enough meat to sink your teeth into. And I'm not even talking of spices yet!

(She continues changing channels impatiently with the remote

control. Mouth munching mechanically.)

Football, Pop-shows, Badminton! Rock bands! God, those undernourished modern Malay boys and their scruffy hairdos - SHORT HAIR! Oh Rahmat, really! Half-baked Dramas. Not another sobbing scene!
They just don't make programs for mature women, do they?

(She still plays with the remote control.)

What have we got here?

KUALI! Our authentic local cuisine lesson at its unadulterated, spicy best!

(She chuckles gleefully and curls herself into a cozy bundle.)

O fo! *Masak Ayam Percek* à la Kelantan! *Aku punya speciality ini!* Let's see how they do it!

(She scoffs another mouthful of petit fours as she recites word for word the instructions of the recipe.)

2 kg *ayam di potong......* *(in response to TV)*

Colouring!

Chicken cubes!

(Half way she begins to protest over the 'authenticity' of the recipe.)

Heh! *apa ini!...*

(Continues persevering with 'learning'...but gives up as the travesty becomes too much for her.)

Ini bukan authentic! *Ini* recipe short-cut! Not in my time Miss.

We wouldn't dare put chicken cubes in our *ayam percek.*

We'd always give the poulet the full treatment. *(Chuckles)*

That's the least it deserves! How can people get away with so much faking!

Call me old-fashioned but I always say that you should live in a place before you try to meddle with the culture.

Especially an art as intimate as cooking!

Take me, for instance. I've lived on the East Coast for the best part of my life. Love the place. Love the culture. You name it. Kota Baru, Besut, Dungun right down to Kuala Trengganu. I've lived there. I know it all, from their Makyong, their *dikir barat,* their best picnic spots right down to their cooking!

Yes, Miss. Please don't tell me that they put chicken cubes in their *Ayam Percek* à la Kelantan!

It's a recipe for suburbia, if you ask me!

Just like those Mat Sallehs who put bananas and carrots into their curry pot. What a travesty!

Well, I think I've had enough of the idiot box for the day. I've yet to come to terms with the country's lowest common denominator.

(She switches off the TV in disgust. By another remote control she switches on the compact disk player. A Debussy waltz fills the room. Deena puts down her spectacles, heaves herself

up and pours herself a drink. She lights a cigar. She inhales deeply, puffing and enjoying the smoke. She waltzes and swans gracefully, imagining that she is at a ball. She handles the cigar deftly like an expert. She lands on a chair puffing lightly. Music decreases to a comfortable volume. She ruminates but finally decides to amuse herself with a deck of cards. She plays solitaire. She has another drink. The following monologue is delivered as she plays solitaire. It is as if Deena is speaking to her 'other self'.)

When you get to my age. When your husband has passed over and your children have grown up and have their own lives to worry about. When there're only a few more of your genuine friends around that haven't dropped off the twig. When there's a senseless war on one side and cancer on the other - a woman my age, and size *(she pops in a chocolate)* appreciates God's little mercies.

She has at least the good ol' Scotch and the cigar to keep her company. And *(another morsel),* food! Can't forget that.

It'll be the death of you Mrs MacIntosh, the Doctor says. Got to keep the weight down. High cholesterol, high blood-pressure, lung cancer... hypertension.

Well, Doctor Nathan. That's me! So there!

It's my choice Doctor, I always say to him.

When I go, it'll be quick and short.

You know I hate fuss. Those sobbing scenes aren't for me, not even over my dead body.

I come to you simply because of the pain.

Physical pain is loathsome to me.

I can cope with anything but pain. So it's up to you Doctor to eliminate this - this 'pain' that I have in my kidney. If not my liver. My chest. If not my chest, my stomach.
That's what you're for, Pet! I tell him.

(She shifts her concentration to the cards and inhales on her cigar with relish. She devotes a few seconds of interest to the way the solitaire is developing. But she soon continues where she has left off.)

But please don't tell me to stop drinking, smoking or eating. What has a woman to live for, may I ask?

You can devote only so much time to God and Art.

So what is one to do with the rest of the eighteen hours of one's waking life?

I live for the joy of Food! Oh, I can go on about food like an art lover about Picasso's Guernica!

I've learnt to appreciate food more than I could ever appreciate Opera.

Opera makes me all sad and morose in the end. It brings me right back to my own life.

Let's face it! The whole human existence is sad. There is a lot of truth in the Buddhist view that life equals suffering!

Life is tragic, let's face it!

Nothing, I say, is equal to the pleasure of good food.

When my dear James was around I may not have entirely agreed, but after he went...*(a puff of the old cigar smoke)*, a lady has to have her pleasures...

Pritikin, Scarsdale, Protein diets - you name it, I've been through it.
It was no use! Even worse was the guilt that it was causing me.

The guilt that I was letting myself down was making me sick more than anything else! I was simply fighting against nature!

Well... that was years ago - before I came to a more positive realisation that the Food Goddess has chosen me as her vehicle for incarnation.

(She laughs infectiously at her own vision of herself.)

It's a simple earthy philosophy of life: You don't let a habit lick you. You lick the habit!

(She continues laughing uproariously at her own pun. It makes her cough. It is not a healthy cough and she starts to look for her pills.)

How dear old James loved his cigar... dear God, I always loved the smell...

(She identifies the pills and swallows the multi-coloured pills one by one.)

One for the blood pressure, one for the heart and one for the kidney!

(She continues with her solitaire.)

Oh yes, there are people who still remember the dinners that I gave them ten years ago! Those were some dinners! Heavenly assortments, painstakingly prepared, one course after the other.

Food fit for the Gods, I'd say... Never hurried. Presented impeccably... that's part of the enjoyment.

Oh those lurid flourishes of show-off cooks are not my style.

The presentation of good food is like getting the right stage effects in a good play.

It's a real art, knowing how to invest the table with an aura of anticipation, the teasing and whetting one more taste bud and the mollifying of the palate, and only then - the reward! The whiff of the heavenly aroma to bring out the right juices and *voila*! It's right there, ready before you.

There is something sexual about the partaking of good food. There's always some teasing and foreplay before the actual act of mastication. And of course, it helps to be in the right company!

Like James and I. We were made for each other. I mean sex of course...

It should be a great celebration of the senses!

My dinner parties are never one of those vulgar food binges. I would never stuff my guests with heavy Indian curries or rich Italian pasta and pastries in one go.

And before you know it, everyone is ready to go home.

All that preparation! NO! Not me.

It would be against my philosophy.

I know too well the heavy and bloated feeling of eating too much, too quickly. All over too soon!

Nothing one can do after a binge but be a bore!

I've always thought food and sex have a lot in common.

Those "wham-bang-thank-you-ma'am" experiences are not for me.

(The phone rings. She doesn't hurry but puts down her cigar, triumphantly lifts up the last card and finally her spectacles. Only then she grabs the mobile phone.)

Who can this be, I wonder.

Hello. Hello darling! No darling! You are not disturbing me. I've just had my siesta. No pet. I usually need only a catnap. Yes. I feel wonderful. What? No, not at all. Be glad to.

Dinner at home? Your husband's business directors? Tonight? Wonderful menu darling! What great choice!

Yes, darling, spicy baked chicken is my favourite dish - my forte, Dulcie...

(Pause) The chilli and coriander should be in the ratio of two to one. Yes, fresh of course. You know I never use those prepared concoctions! *(She laughs)*

In that case, you should've consulted the cook book, not me. *(Pause, sceptical and recriminating)*

But darling, darling! The poulet should have been marinated and refrigerated, and left there for at least sixteen hours. That means preparing the bird last night. *(Pause)* The amah has not taken it out of the freezer, yet?

Microwave? But the spices will not have the chance to get

right in, darling! Otherwise the chicken will be like those newly arrived socialites - shallow and totally unsavoury inside.

Tell you what Dulcie, dear. Do you remember that wonderful restaurant I took you to lunch about a month ago? Remember how you loved the food? Why don't... Wait a second. *(She looks for a telephone number)* The number is 293 0397. They are experienced caterers. Yes, you can depend on them. Yes darling. It'll save you all that bother...

No darling. I am not free tonight.

I am taking the new Swiss ambassador and his wife to the Hakka restaurant. I thought it would be a nice change from those boring formal receptions.

Thank you for the invitation anyway. Some other time, perhaps.

Bye.

(Deena puts down the phone casually. Obviously she has had similar phone calls from her friend.)

Poor Dulcie! Wonderful friend, but I'm afraid she hasn't got it in her.

I always say, you can have all the money in the world darling, but if you haven't got it by this time - you may as well stick to the safe formula.

Leave the higher experience for the bright sparks like me.

It's difficult to pinpoint - what makes one person able to create something great out of nothing, and another who has everything, somehow come out with - er - nothing, in whatever she does.

There are just a few of us 'genuine' socialites - I cringe at that tinsel label they brand us 'ladies of leisure'. There are those who have that 'star' quality - the rest are the lesser constellations - the ones who are always organising or running to the next fashion show - inevitably behind the fashion, of course. And, oh, those loud and busy ones. The louder they are the more you can be sure that their marriages are not going quite right.

The way they flaunt their wealth! Huge massive mansions that look like oil rigs in the night. Fleets of cars with stickers of all the clubs they belong to splattered all over the windscreen. Big, noisy buffet parties - catered for, of course... all the usual signs of being too rich, too quickly...

But they don't fool me. I only need to have one look at the paintings they've got, their furniture or their selection of music, I'd know exactly where they stand...

And, of course, they've all recently discovered ART...

Nothing like the quiet, classical style of the Indonesian women we used to meet.

Yes, I've seen the way this country has come up in the world.

It's never been a great cultural centre. More like a business convention centre. Businessmen come and they go. Like the monsoons - down through the ages.

Now it's convention fever. They want more hotels, restaurants, entertainments and massage-parlours...

Really, the only culture they can really appreciate here is the FOOD culture!

(Deena gets more excited. She lights another cigar.)

One era of commercial development after another! Now I see it in the big cities and all over those massive advertising billboards. The high-rise condominiums. The shopping complexes...

I call it the TV era - Triumph of Vulgarity era! With a fascinating Malaysian flavour...

(Deena puffs out thick cigar smoke.)

Just look at our lights in the city. There's no difference between the seafood restaurants along Old Klang Road and the city centre! Must we have the whole city lit up in such a tarty manner?

When in doubt - bring out the lights! It never fails to please the politicians, of course!

(By this time Deena is walking up and down the stage. Waving whatever material or things she can get hold of...)

I remember the *Dataran* when the Malayan Flag was raised, holding back my tears thinking of poor old James, amidst shouts of *MERDEKA!*

What has happened to the *Dataran* now? The most sacred ground in KL ...Mass extravaganzas!!! The symbol for the lowest common denominator, again!

Call me old-fashioned, darling. But I simply can't associate it with the Days of Independence, the days of history in the making!

I've nothing against rock bands and the hoi-polloi having fun - but there should also be a time and place for excellence!

A place of distinction. And taste... A place for people like me!

Where do you find that in Kuala Lumpur?

But the country has its charms. Or else I wouldn't be here, darling. Would I?

(Deena resigns herself back to the sofa. She pours herself another drink and catches her breath. A keroncong is heard in the distance. She goes to a drawer and retrieves a hidden photo. She smiles and admires the photograph nostalgically.)

As I said, you can devote so much time to God, Art and Food. God forbid, I never went looking for it like some of my more desperate friends. Eventually, a lady like me must have her little titillations - well, when the opportunity knocked, who was I to refuse? I felt like the Little Red Riding Hood who finally said to the Big Bad Wolf: "Food! Food! Food! - That's all you ever think of - doesn't anybody fuck here anymore!" *(Deena shrieks at her own joke.)*

That was only twelve years ago! There I was, a lonely widow - the kids in college overseas...

Yes, I wonder what's happened to my Boy? Where he went.

I didn't take him too seriously at first. It had been so long since I had had a lover. But then, slowly, I became more and more besotted with him.

Of course, I was careful. No-one knew about him. At least as far as I know, but you never know in KL.

You only have to fart in KL and they'd hear it in PJ.

My beautiful Boy! *(Deena sighs and goes all soft and 'motherly'.)*

Those Malay boys, they have such charm and grace!

But what vanity!

When I think of how we first met! At a reception! He was one of the waiters helping with the catering. After a few opening gambits, we knew we had a lot in common, improbable as it would seem.

We had the same points of reference - COOKING!

God, I was bold! Invited him home after the reception. Discreetly, of course. I almost ran out of ideas and excuses for more receptions! It was SO exciting. That boy filled my life! And I can tell you, by that time, was I starved!

What a change! What lovely, slow languorous afternoons. And the mornings! I was astonished at myself! I thought I was a passionate woman with James!

It was so delicious and naughty with Ismail.

Oh Go-od! I have said his name! Well, why not?

Mrs Stone - you and your Roman Spring. Eat your heart out!

Mine was the Malaysian Wet of Mrs MacIntosh!

But it didn't last. I just wasn't lusty enough for my young Arjuna. He was insatiable!

I had to let him go. My mirror told me so. I bought him a gold bracelet and gave him a small settlement, I was so grateful.

But I am glad we did it. I needed to know that other side of love.

Even my cooking got much better after Ismail... much more

SAUCY! *(She laughs uproariously.)*

After he left all I did was eat. I had to fill the void! Just ballooned and no-one could guess why! Personally, I think it was a fair exchange. So there!
Another éclair, Mrs MacIntosh? Don't mind if I do!

(Deena helps herself to an éclair. She munches slowly and continues talking.)

Feeling peckish Deena?

Mmm... lunch was rather austere today. No wonder I wasn't able to sink into my usual siesta ...A little bit of sustenance before the serious food tonight wouldn't harm you Deena...

Oh God! I just remembered. I didn't stock the fridge! There's nothing in the food box! What a disaster! How does a dame in distress cope with such an emergency?

Call the take-away pizza! Of course...!

(She calls the pizza shop. She has memorised the number.)

Hello. Pizza Hut? Ya. *Tolong bawa saya satu pizza -* Medium. *Ya. Saya mau* Carbonara Neopolitana. *Ya. Itu* anchovie *kasi lebih. Itu cendawan tidak mau.*

Awak guna itu cendawan tin. Tidak bagus. Saya tidak suka.

OK. Mrs MacIntosh. 25, Jalan Kia Peng.

Sekarang. Dalam berapa minit? Bagus. Saya tunggu...

(She puts down the phone.)

Don't get me wrong! I claim myself a connoisseur of food.

That doesn't mean I don't indulge in take-aways once in a while. It's good for you! All those intellectual men love pornography and patronise the whore-house now and then, don't they?

A craving to wallow in those cheesy, saucy, soggy foodstuffs now and then, is a perfectly natural indulgence. To deny it would be unwise...

I always know when my system needs a MacDonald Cheese-Burger or a Kentucky. Now it's pizza!

I call it the pull of opposites! So there!

By the time you get to be my age, you get to know all about the workings of your body. The safety valves and mechanisms that switch on and off. They compensate for the imbalance in hormones, I suppose.

Better than breaking out in rashes, or worse still, I know some people who develop kinky complexes...

When I'm in the dumps I aim straight for the kitchen. It's like a magnetic chamber.

I was in the kitchen when James was murdered. Elbow deep in flour when it all happened. *(She chuckles.)*
(The whole of this conversation is done almost facetiously. It really disguises one of the most chilling and grisly experiences for Deena.)

Yes I was baking my poor darling James his favourite whole-meal loaf when the Communists stormed the house. *(She chuckles.)*

Everybody knows that Deena's bread is unsurpassable. Nobody bakes bread the way I do. By George, when I prepare my bread, I go into a trance. It's like the whole force wells up in me. All my energy and being goes into that bread!

(Deena begins describing, in the most intense manner the whole procedure of bread-making. She clears the table of the deck of cards and glasses. Lights herself a cigar and mimes the action of pouring water in the flour, kneading the dough, etc. She's already perspiring from the excitement.)

Four little vermins, they were... All I heard was the scurrying of the servants. And Bang! *(Giggles)*

There weren't that many of us. The two amahs, the gardener, the driver and the security guard. The old security guard was knocked off easily enough. We found his body by the alamanda bush - his throat slit from one ear to the other.

We just never expected the attack. Poor James was one of the earliest victims in the country.

I'll never forget... I had told the amah to prepare the yeast-blend. I always like to do the kneading myself. It gives me an Earth Goddess-like sense of well-being, of giving life I suppose.

Sleeves rolled up, elbows deep in flour - there I was kneading to my heart's content.
(Long silence.)

Really, bread is just dough that has turned sour, and baked. That's all there is to it.

But whether your bread is going to have a crispy crust with a golden colour, soft crumbs and taste heavenly or come out insipid - Well, that's another matter.

The dough was just getting to be smooth and elastic when "BANG"! The door of the kitchen was almost torn off its hinges.

(Deena chuckles hysterically...At this point, the soft sound-special of kneading is heard. The squelching and squashing of wet flour being kneaded increases in volume as the drama increases in tension.)

Poor James shot out of the door - followed by three of the bastards. The two amahs were screaming!

They kept thrashing and thrashing him. Used bamboo poles to stab him. And God knows what else. He didn't have a chance. *(Laughs as she kneads her 'dough' more vigorously.)* They were slapping and poking him. Blood spurting everywhere.

Then they went after the younger, prettier amah. I suppose I looked as unappetising as the lump of dough in front of me. Whatever the reason, they went past me like I wasn't there.

The animal simply lowered his trousers, pinned the poor girl down and raped her, there and then on the kitchen floor!

I was completely hypnotised! Struck dumb! Petrified. I couldn't even raise a finger! I couldn't even scream. My jaws were locked. The shock of it all!

Somehow I was completely spared! It was as if my fairy god-mother was protecting me. As if the Food Goddess had changed me into a lump of dough during that commotion. And that suspended limbo became the most unconsummated part of my life! I know I shall be forever born again to complete baking that unfinished bread!

I would've been better off raped and killed with my James...

There I was, in my dishevelled state, my hands limp, elbow-deep in wholemeal flour. One of them held my James against the oven while the other pounded and pounded on him! *(Deena simulates a pounding motion with her dough.)* By that time I suppose he'd passed out. Then they dragged him like a battered rag doll, out of the back door. I hope he was dead by then... *(Pause)* They found his body three days later, in a peat swamp, mutilated beyond recognition... *(Deena suppresses her real emotions, alternating between chuckling and weeping in an almost hysterical manner...The 'kneading' sound-special slowly decreases in volume to zero.)*

(After this tense section, Deena is totally exhausted. She makes the motion of cleaning her hands. She wipes her perspiration. Stumbles to the chaise-lounge and drops off.)

(We then hear her theme music - a Debussy waltz. The 'kneading' sound is again inserted. The waltz is suddenly interrupted by the sudden opening of a door. Voices. Screaming. The murder of her husband is re-enacted in its goriest vocal terror. We hear at the same time, the thud, thud, thud kneading of dough - magnified a hundred times. The thudding remains. The rest of the sounds disappear...)

(There is a sound of a doorbell. Deena wakes up...)

I think that must be the pizza man...

Black out.

End

THE RETURN
K.S. Maniam

K.S. Maniam's classic novel depicts the experiences of an immigrant community in Peninsula Malaysia before and after Independence in 1957. It documents the bewilderment and loss of bearings felt within a once secure world coming to an end in political and cultural fragmentation.

Skoob *PACIFICA* Series No. 2001
ISBN 1 871438 04 7 P'bk 208 pp   GBP £5.99

AVAILABLE FROM ALL GOOD BOOKSHOPS OR ORDER FROM
SKOOB TWO WITH CREDIT CARD.   TEL: 071 405 0030.
POST FREE IN UK.

WAYS OF EXILE
Poems from the First Decade
Wong Phui Nam

'THESE POEMS NEED TO BE WRITTEN. They are of a time, of a place, of a people who find themselves having to live by institutions and folkways which are not of their heritage, having to absorb the manners of languages not their own.'

Wong Phui Nam
How the Hills Are Distant

Skoob *PACIFICA* Series No. 2002

ISBN 1 871438 09 8   P'bk 176 pp   GBP £5.99

AVAILABLE FROM ALL GOOD BOOKSHOPS OR ORDER FROM SKOOB TWO WITH CREDIT CARD. TEL: **071 405 0030**. POST FREE IN UK.

IN A FAR COUNTRY
K.S. Maniam

A new novel from K.S. Maniam. *In a Far Country* continues his layered multicultural perspective on the themes of material progress, ancient community, and sense of belonging. The story leads on from the period of *The Return* to cover the quarter of a century from the 1960's onwards.

Skoob *PACIFICA* Series No. 2003
ISBN 1 871438 14 4 P'bk 224 pp GBP £5.99

SKOOB PACIFICA ANTHOLOGY NO.1
S.E.Asia Writes Back !
Contemporary writings of the Pacific Rim

In Memory of Lee Kok Liang by Syd Harrex
Preface by Ike Ong
Introduction by John McRae

* ShirleyGeok-lin Lim
* Thor Kah Hoong
* Karim Raslan
* Robert Yeo
* Arthur Yap
* Philip Jeyaretnam
* Alfred A. Yuson
* Michael Wilding
* Jan Kemp
* Chin Woon Ping
* Paul Sharrad
* K.S. Maniam
* Kee Thuan Chye
* Latiff Mohidin
* Cecil Rajendra
* Leong Liew Geok
* Lee Tzu Pheng
* Kirpal Singh
* Siew -Yue Killingley
* Anne Brewster
⸴ Malachi Edwin
* Wong Phui Nam
* John McRae
* Ramli Ibrahim
* Lee Kok Liang
* C.W. Watson
* Pira Sudham
* Alan Durant
* Annie Greet
* Yukio Mishima
* Vikram Seth

Skoob *PACIFICA* Series No. 2000
ISBN 1 871438 19 5
P'bk 432 pp GBP £5.99

Available from all good bookshops or order from SKOOB TWO with credit card. Tel: 071 405 0030. Post free in UK.

Contemporary writings of the Pacific rim

SKOOB PACIFICA ANTHOLOGY No.1

NOBEL LAUREATES
* Derek Walcott
* Wole Soyinka
* Yasunari Kawabata

Skoob *PACIFICA* Anthology No: 2
THE PEN IS MIGHTIER THAN THE SWORD
Forthcoming Winter 1993

Part One
New Writings of the Pacific Rim

Part Two
Malaysian/Singaporean Prose in English:
Main feature: The books of **Chin Kee Onn.**

Part Three
Other literatures of the Pacific Rim:
Ashcroft, Griffiths & Tiffin: *Post-colonial reconstructions: Literature, Meaning and Value and Post-colonialism as a Reading Strategy* (excerpts from *The Empire Writes Back, Theory and Practice in Post-colonial Literatures*)
and other studies of South East Asian literatures.

Part Four
The Nobel Laureates:
Josef Brodsky * Czeslaw Milosz (with the *Witness of Poetry :* The Charles Eliot Norton Lectures 1981-2)
Jean-Paul Sartre (*The Writer and His Language* and Citation, Address and Refusal)
Nadine Gordimer * Naguib Mahfouz
Gabriel Marquez * Octavio Paz.

Part Five
Literary Features:
Vikram Seth's Journey Continues:
Chapter 2 *Heaven Lake* and Chapter 3 *An Eastward Loop* (excerpts from *From Heaven Lake, Travels through Sinkiang and Tibet*)
V.S. Naipaul's Travels through Malaysia:
First Conversations With Shafi: The Journey Out of Paradise.
(excerpts from *Among the Believers: An Islamic Journey*)

SKOOB **Pacifica** SERIES

Skoob Pacifica Anthology
is a quarterly publication featuring
contemporary writings of the Pacific Rim

The first issue
SKOOB PACIFICA ANTHOLOGY No. 1
S.E. Asia Writes Back !

Subscription of Five issues:
UK GBP £20 post free
Elsewhere GBP £25 post free surface mail

Subscription enquiries to Skoob Books Publishing Ltd,
11A-17 Sicilian Avenue, off Southampton Row and
Bloomsbury Square, London WC1A 2 QH
Fax: 71-404 -4398
Cheques payable to Skoob Books Publishing Ltd.
I enclose a cheque for GBP £_____

Please debit my Access/Visa/Amex account
expiry date_____

Signature _____

Card No.

Name   _____
Address _____
         _____
         _____